Railways in Profile Se

BRITISH RAILWAY VANS

Compiled by G. Gamble

CHEONA PUBLICATIONS

Reprinted March 1998

ISBN 1 900298 03 1

Production, design and setting by
Print-Rite, The Willows, School Lane,
Stadhampton, Oxford OX44 7TR

Printed by Alpha Print, Crawley, Oxon.

Published by:-
Cheona Publications,
39 The Avenue, Chinnor,
Oxfordshire OX9 4PD

The Railways in Profile Series.

> No.1 British Railway Wagons. Opens and Hoppers *(published)*
> No.2 Great Western Stations. *(published)*
> No.3 British Railway Vans. *(this volume)*

In preparation:-

> British Railway Brake Vans, Cattle Vans, Horseboxes and Special Vehicles.
> British Railway Air Braked Stock.
> British Railway Air Braked Stock - Private Owner and Ferry Vans.
> British Railway early Tank Wagons and other early Private Owner Wagons.
> British Railway Engineering Departmental Stock.
> British Railway Lineside Structures and Fittings.

Plus others!

If you have any material suitable for any of the above volumes then please contact the publisher at the address above.

Acknowledgements

Such a work as this relies heavily on the availability of photographs and so grateful thanks are extended to all who have made such material available to me. They have been indicated by initials and are: E.B. - Eric Bruton, B.D. - Brian Daniels, D.L. - David Larkin, R.C. - Roger Carpenter, H.F.W. - Frank Wheeler (*via* Roger Carpenter), G.G. - Geoff Gamble, B.R./A.B. - British Railways (A.Beaton collection), A.B. - A.Beaton collection, P.B. - Peter Bossom, R.S. - Roger Speller, T.M. - Terry Murphy, C.R. - Colour-Rail, P.W. - Pete Watson, S.C. - Stan Cartwright (*via* Roger Carpenter), L. - Lens of Sutton, B.R./D.L. - British Railways (D.Larkin collection), A.S. - Alan Searle.
I would also like to thank Colin Judge for his help in design and production of this book and David Larkin for checking the proofs.

Preface

This book sets the scene post-nationalisation by showing some of the inherited freight vehicles at work on British Railways and also illustrates some of the new designs launched into service by BR. It is intended to act as an aid to modellers and others who need photographs to assist in the assembly and alteration of the many plastic/etched brass/cast kits now available. As much detail as possible has been included in the captions of the photographs but to save repetition, livery details are those given in the introductory section unless otherwise stated. These can generally be resolved into fitted (vacuum braked stock) or unfitted, where braking was independent on each vehicle and could not be controlled by the driver or guard when the train was in motion.

INTRODUCTION

On 1st January, 1948, the 'Big Four' (Great Western; London Midland and Scottish; London and North Eastern and Southern Railways) were nationalised to form British Railways.

The new body inherited thousands of freight vehicles of varying designs from the 'Big Four' as well as some from private owners.

As with open wagons, some of which were covered in **'Railways in Profile No. 1'**, BR found itself in possession of a wide range of designs of van in varying condition. The 'Big Four' designs were perpetuated by BR, with modifications in many cases, and work was implemented on a BR standard van design. The first of these vehicles built to diagram 1/208, were introduced in 1951 and a range of other designs were produced by modifying this diagram. Diagram 1/208 produced the largest number of vans (19063, built between 1951 and 1958.)

A 17ft 6in underframe on a 10ft wheelbase chassis was the basis of all British Railways - built general goods vans and the vast majority had automatic vacuum brake gear. The body had pressed-steel ends with wooden sides which had hinged doors. The cupboard door style of the GWR/SR was preferred to the sliding style of the LMS/LNE which took a lot of strength to move. The disadvantage of cupboard doors was the difficulty of opening them alongside buildings.

Diagram and Lot numbers

British Railways introduced three diagram books to cover freight stock. Book 1 was for ordinary vehicles, Book 2 for specially built vehicles and Book 3 for containers. The pages in each book were numbered from 1 and thus a van with a diagram number 1/213 would be found on page 213 of Book 1.

The same diagram was often used to build batches of the same design of van over a period of time and so a lot number was allocated to each batch built e.g. Diagram 1/213, Lot 2855 - a batch of 750 ventilated goods vans with plywood sides and doors numbered B772201 to B772950 and built at BR Ashford Works in 1956.

Note: Diagram, Lot and Running numbers have been given whenever possible but the reader is reminded that variations did occur within a particular lot in some cases.

Numbering

Pre-Grouping Company Stock - retained the original number but this was prefixed by a single letter from the original company letters, (the latter were still retained on the original builder's plates but only the appropriate letter was picked out in white).

Ex-GWR stock adopted the prefix letter	"	'W'
Ex-LMS	"	'M'
Ex-LNER	"	'E'
Ex-SR	"	'S'

British Railways Built Stock - for general use had the prefix 'B' followed by a number selected from a batch allocated to the particular class of vehicle involved.

British Railways Built Stock - for the Engineers' department used the prefix 'DB'. Stock transferred from general use to this department was given the 'DB' prefix on the body - often before the original number which was retained on the original wagon plate on the solebars.

Liveries

Non-Fitted Stock - (not fitted with vacuum brakes) was given a grey body, black solebars, headstocks and below, with a black or grey roof. Lettering was in white on black panels.

Fitted Stock - (vacuum braked) was painted bauxite (a red/brown colour) for the body with black solebars, headstocks and below and a black or grey roof. White lettering was applied directly onto the bauxite. Vacuum pipes were colour-coded :- white for through-piped stock and red for fully fitted.

The original colours did vary, especially the grey, with dust, rust and general grime of service much altering the base applied colours.

It should be noted that there was great variation in the painting of the chassis - sometimes the solebars were painted the same colour as the body and similarly the headstocks - this was more commonly seen on the fitted stock.

Insulated Stock - (for the conveyance of perishables like fish and meat). Insulated vans and containers were painted stone which was soon superseded by white, both with black lettering. From 1964 this body colour was changed to a pale blue colour - ice blue, and white lettering was applied instead of black.

Ventilated meat vans and containers were crimson lake with yellow lettering (passenger stock livery) but many were soon painted bauxite with white lettering. All other vans including non-insulated fish vans, were standard colours.

Engineers' Department Stock - was initially painted black with yellow lettering. This was later replaced by an olive green body colour.

Lettering - was similar to the style used from the 1930's by the pre-grouping companies. The number was painted on the lower left part of the body. If the vehicle had a code name this was painted above the number.

On the lower right of the body the tare weight was often noted. The solebar (the side frame of the chassis) carried the wagon/van plate and also, as appropriate, a builder's plate and a repairer's plate. The former plate was generally to the left and often close to it, would be the clip to hold the vehicle load label, which was removed when the vehicle reached its destination.

From circa 1964, all lettering was grouped together at the lower left of the vehicle side and it was surrounded by a white line.

As BR standard van designs were introduced telegraphic code names were issued. Some of the names used were; PALVAN, SHOCVAN and later VANWIDE and VANFIT.

TOPS - from 1972 the TOPS (Total Operations Processing System) was introduced where every vehicle on BR was given a computer recorded number and a 3-letter code. This system enabled an exact log to be kept of how many vehicles there were on the railway and their whereabouts. These codes were added to vehicles with either early or late styles of lettering. *See plate 89.*

TOPS Numbering - each vehicle had its own fleet number, which if it was a new generation privately owned vehicle was preceded by capital letters derived from the name of the owner to clearly characterise it.

TOPS Code letters

1. The first letter identifies the vehicle type:-

B = Bogie bolster, plate and rail wagons.	O = Open goods wagons.
C = Brake vans, covered hoppers and gunpowder vans.	R = Runner wagons, barrier wagons and diesel brake tenders.
F = Flat wagons including carflats, conflats and freightliner wagons.	S = Non-bogie steel carryin wagons.
H = Hopper wagons.	U = Miscellaneous unconverte vacuum-braked wagon types.
I = Internationally owned stock.	V = Vans.
J = Bogie coil wagons.	X = Specially constructed vehicles.
K = Non- bogie coil wagons.	Y = Departmental wagons.
M = Mineral wagons.	Z = Departmental wagons.

2. *The second letter identifies which group the vehicle belongs to within its type.*
3. *The third letter indicates the type of braking the vehicle has viz:*

A = Air braked.
B = Air braked with vacuum brake through pipe.
O = Hand brake only.
P = Vacuum brake through pipe.
V = Vacuum braked.
X = Dual air and vacuum brakes.

Van Labels

Each van making a journey had to carry an appropriate label in a clip on the solebar. The label gave the date, sender, point of origin, destination, route, van letter and number, weight, description of load and consignee. *(See inside back cover).*

Plate 1. No.119 'Shaka Salt' 10T salt van with steel solebars and wooden headstocks fitted with spindle buffers. The horizontally planked wooden body has prominent wooden end posts and large steel corner plates. It is unfitted with independent brake gear. The body was painted mid blue with white lettering, the lower bodyside band being dark blue. Photographed at Birmingham Snow Hill, 1958.   R.C.

Plate 2. E75366 is an ex-LNER diagram 214, 12T INSUL-FISH van built 1949-1950 at BR Faverdale, Darlington Works. It has a 15ft wheelbase steel chassis with LNER style eight shoe vacuum brakegear, disc wheels and self contained buffers. The left hand axlebox is LNER pattern, the right hand one is a BR plate front type. Being designed for possible passenger train working, it also has steam pipes. Livery was all white aluminium plated plywood body, black solebars and below and black lettering when photographed at Birmingham Suffolk Street Goods depot, 1959.   R.C.

Plate 3. E75474 is a 12T INSUL-FISH van of LNER diagram 214, (E75000-E75599) like the previous plate in many ways. The small lettering to the left of the door reads 'NOT TO WORK BETWEEN/TONBRIDGE AND BATTLE/VIA ROBERTSBRIDGE/SOUTHERN REGION'. Photographed at Birmingham New Street station, 1951. S.C./R.C.

Plate 4. E87093 is a 12T INSUL-FISH van of the first BR design (E87000-E87499), based on the LNER diagram 214. The main difference between the two designs is the use of roller bearings here. By this time these vans should have been painted in ice blue livery but most merely had an ice blue panel with new lettering and remained dirty white. The large blue spot gave the name 'Blue Spot Fish Vans' to these roller bearing-fitted vehicles. The white lettering on the blue patch reads 'TO WORK BETWEEN/ABERDEEN & KINGS CROSS'; solebars and below are black (but not headstocks). Photographed at Leamington Spa General station, September 1964. H.F.W./R.C.

Plate 5. (AD) E75415 is an ex-LNER diagram 214, 12T INSUL-FISH van. With the disappearance of much of the fish traffic from the railways by the late 1960's, many such vans found new uses and this one has been modified to work as a boiler van for carriage heating. It has extra bracing and split axleboxes but its disc wheels, eight shoe vacuum brakes and self contained buffers are similar features to the three previous plates. Livery was Rail Blue with white lettering when captured on film at Oxford MPD on 4th August, 1977. G.G.

Plate 6. E88005 is a BR (second design - E87500-E88057), former 12T INSUL-FISH van with similar characteristics to the one depicted on the rear cover in colour. Classified NRV it was in weathered Express Parcels service livery of Rail Blue with white lettering when photographed at Didcot, October 1979. B.D.

Plate 7. (CD)M299034 is an ex-LMS 7T gunpowder van built to diagram D1665, lot No. 709, (20 built in Derby Works in 1933, M299031-M299050). It has been uprated to 11T by BR but still has its original split axleboxes and spindle buffers. Note the vacuum pipe, (this van was built unfitted with a through vacuum pipe), screw couplings and tiebars. The cast plate on the door reads: 'NOTICE/NO UNAUTHORISED PERSON/IS ALLOWED/TO OPEN THESE DOORS'. Photographed at Temple Mills, 20th March 1980.

B.D.

Plate 8. B887083 is an 11T gunpowder van built to diagram 1/260, lot No. 2689, (35 vans, B887065-B887099) at BR Swindon Works in 1955. It is based on GWR diagram Z4 and is only 10ft 6ins high with a 9ft 0in wheelbase chassis and a 16ft 6ins long body (over headstocks). Of all steel construction with lockable doors, it has vacuum brakes, plate front axleboxes, tie bars, spindle buffers and Instanter couplings. Photographed at Doncaster, Summer 1969.

D.L.

Plate 9. M33224 is an ex-MR/LMS 10T unfitted goods van, diagram D363, which when photographed in 1959 still showed most of its original features (including spindle buffers, springs, axleboxes and brake gear as well as split spoked wheels). It has wooden solebars and headstocks and its horizontally planked wooden body has characteristic Midland style external wooden bracing. In use here as a static store. R.C.

Plate 10. M160267 is an unfitted, ex-LMS 12T ventilated goods van built to diagram D1832A at Wolverton Works in 1929. The two part corrugated end is clearly seen and it has two rows of two torpedo vents on the roof. Note the Morton reversing clutch and the strengthening strip on the V-hanger, the split axleboxes and the four shoe brakes. The paint date on the solebar is 17-2-49 - only a short while before it was photographed at St Albans City. Livery was recorded as LMS bauxite with white lettering - a result of old stocks of paint being used up - next time round it would get the BR pale grey no doubt!   E.B.

Plate 11. M523422 is an ex-LMS 12T van built by the SR to their diagram 1455, (LMS diagram D2078, lot No. 1373, M523290-M523539 [250 vans]) in 1944. It has the mixed planking used on all late SR vans and its chassis has four shoe vacuum brakes, tie bars, open front axleboxes and replacement buffers. Vacuum braked by BR circa 1959. Photographed at Marshmoor in the early 1970's.   T.M.

Plate 12. M518972 is an ex-LMS 12T van, with horizontally planked sides and the later three part corrugated ends. It was built to diagram D2039, lot No.1333, (800 vans, M518340-M519139) at Wolverton Works in 1942/43. Built unfitted, it has been vacuum braked by BR circa 1956 along with buffer modifications and has screw couplings, tie bars and split axleboxes. Photographed at Marshmoor in the early 1970's.   T.M.

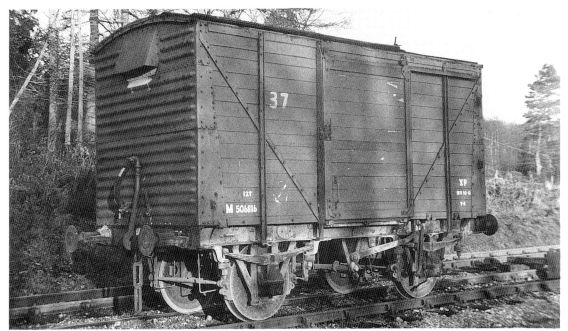

Plate 13. M506816 is a 12T goods van with ventilated three part corrugated ends and horizontally planked wooden sides. It was built to LMS diagram D1897, lot No. 824, (800 vans, M506800-M507599) at Derby Works in 1935 and is seen here in the early 1970's in internal use at Mountfield Gypsum mines near Battle in Sussex. It has eight shoe vacuum brake gear, a 10ft 0in wheelbase chassis, split axleboxes, three-link couplings and typical LMS J-hanger suspension. Note the short brake lever and the tall vacuum pipes. P.B.

Plate 14. M526208 built to LMS diagram D2108, lot No. 1413, (1350 vans, M525140-M526489) at Wolverton Works in 1944, is a 12T fitted van with plywood body and three part corrugated ends. Note the diagonal bracing, tall vacuum pipes and absence of roof vents. BR perpetuated this design as diagram 1/200 with some modifications to the doors. Photographed at Marshmoor in the early 1970's. T.M.

Plate 15. M39767 is an ex-LMS, diagram D2107, 6T Fish van on a 10ft 6ins wheelbase chassis with four-shoe vacuum brake gear. It has spoked wheels, standard LMS pattern spindle buffers and tall vacuum pipes as well as steam heating pipes. The livery is BR crimson with black ends and the coach style lettering is yellow. X in a circle on the side, indicates that the van has been condemned and will be withdrawn when repairs next fall due. Photographed at Mallaig, 18th June, 1951.   E.B.

Plate 16. M114995 is an ex-LMS 8T refrigerator van built originally to diagram D1672 but later changed to D1672A when its ladder and ice boxes were removed pre-1948. It has a vertically narrow-planked body with flush fitting doors and its steel 9ft 0ins wheelbase chassis has four shoe Morton vacuum brakes (8T vans ran in goods trains, 6T vans to the same design ran in passenger trains). Livery is white with black underframe and lettering. Photographed November 1958.   R.C.

Plate 17. 080132 is an ex-LSWR/SR 10T goods van with the typical LSWR-style outside framing. It has a Fox's pressed steel underframe, split spoked wheels, LSWR spindle buffers and two shoe brakes (the latter being on the side away from the camera). Photographed at Feltham MPD on 25th September, 1963 when in departmental use. R.C.

Plate 18. (D) S 46931 is 10T ex-LBSCR/SR van - SR diagram 1436, built in the early 1900's (the number being transposed from a diagram 1434 van, as happened in several cases on the Isle of Wight). It has a horizontally planked wooden body with vertically planked cupboard doors and the wheelbase of its wooden chassis was 9ft 9ins, being 18ft 4ins over headstocks. Original features include LBSCR pattern axleboxes and four shoe Freighter brakes - it has a through Westinghouse pipe. Photographed in use as a STORES VAN at Ryde St Johns, Isle of Wight, 15th August 1964. R.S.

Plate 19. S48314 is an ex-SR fitted goods van built to diagram 1458. It has even wooden planking to the body, tie rods and a mixture of split type and BR plate front axle boxes. Its brake gear is similar to that in *plate 25.* Photographed at Hoo Junction, Spring 1968.   D.L.

Plate 20. S59972 is a 12T ex-SR standard express goods van having a lot of features in common with *plate 21.* The door and body planking are different - note how the body planking has been externally repaired with wide planks to the right of the door. It has split axleboxes, Morton brake gear and tie rods. Photographed at Strood, Spring 1968.   D.L.

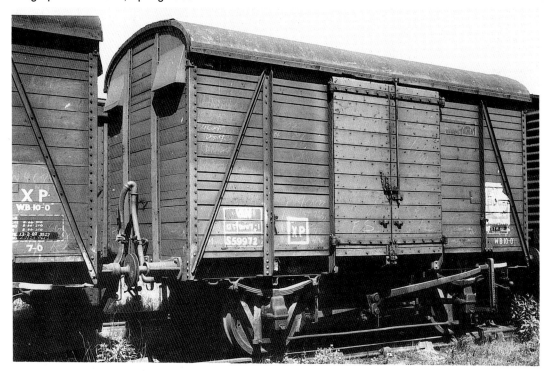

Plate 21. S54239 is an ex-SR 12T van of diagram 1455 - unfitted but vacuum braked by BR circa 1956 (with replacement buffers here). Its body side shows characteristic mixed planking adopted by the SR - from top to bottom:- 1 wide (W), 2 narrow (N), 2W, 2N, 2W, 2N, 2W, 3N, - only disturbed here by repairs to the doors and ends. The body bracing shows up well here. Note the code 'VANFIT'. Photographed at Marshmoor in the early 1970's.   T.M.

Plate 22. S54143 has the same build details as *plate 21* but its body has had considerable replacement planking and note the BR modified buffers (when the van was vacuum braked circa 1956), plate front axleboxes, tie bars, screw couplings and the 'boxed' style of lettering. Photographed at Marshmoor in the early 1970's.   T.M.

Plate 23. S56628 is a 12T ventilated goods van built to SR diagram 1452 (BR diagram 1/202) at Ashford Works and showing similar features to *plate 24* in respect of body construction. It has been vacuum fitted by BR circa 1956, (being built unfitted with Morton four shoe brake gear - like all the SR-built vans to this diagram). Note the low style vacuum pipe and the modified buffers along with the absence of tie bars or rods. Photographed at Hoo Junction, Spring 1968. D.L.

Plate 24. B752698 is a 12T ventilated goods van built to diagram 1/202, lot No. 2062, (440 vans, B752350-B752789) at BR Ashford Works in 1949 and clearly based on the van in the plate above built by the SR. This lot was built with four shoe brake gear (unfitted) and it has open front axleboxes, (the left hand one is lettered LNE), tie bars, spindle buffers and screw couplings. It was vacuum braked circa 1957. As well as having patches on the end, it has recently had a new roof covering. Photographed at Hoo Junction, Spring 1968. D.L.

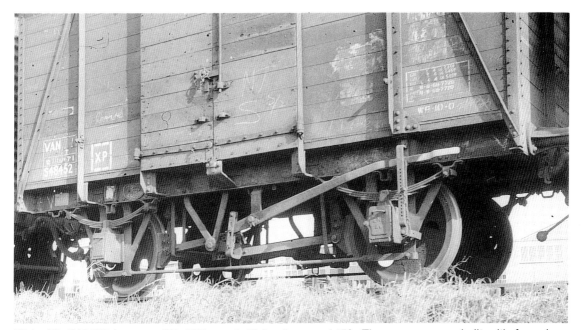

Plate 25. S48452 is an ex-SR 12T van built to diagram 1458. These vans were built with four shoe vacuum brakes with a new control arrangement which is clearly shown here. The vacuum cylinder was offset to one side which led to the large V-hanger left of centre, with a long brake lever having an extra pivot point. Note the tie rod and LNER pattern axleboxes. Photographed at Marshmoor in the early 1970's. T.M.

Plate 26. (D)E951614, with one pair of split spoked wheels and one pair of disc wheels, is an ex-GC/LNER 10T goods van. It has eight shoe vacuum brakes, LNER pattern axleboxes, screw couplings and wooden solebars and headstocks. It has had steps fitted for internal use but is substantially as built when photographed at Darnall Shed, Sheffield, 6th September 1953. H.F.W./R.C.

Plate 27. NE539474 is a 10T box van built by the Metropolitan Carriage & Wagon Co. in 1923 and registered by the Great Central Railway in that year. It has a10ft 6ins wheelbase chassis with eight shoe vacuum brakes, tall vacuum pipes and spoked wheels. Note the door slides open to the left - a Great Central feature. Livery is very weathered red oxide with white lettering. Photographed at St Albans City, 25th May 1949   E.B.

Plate 28. E632438 is an ex-Great Eastern Railway 10T wooden-bodied, ventilated van built by Clayton and Shuttleworth, being registered at Stratford in 1920. It is seen here on 2nd October, 1948 at Kings Langley in fairly new BR bauxite with white lettering, although it is unfitted! Note the unusual planked vent hoods and the racked brake hanger bracket. It has a single brake shoe on each side of its 10ft 6ins wheelbase chassis and is as built, except for the livery and fitting of LNER open front axleboxes.   E.B.

Plate 29. E420542, photographed on 21st May, 1949 at St Albans City, is an ex-Great Northern Railway 8T ventilated, fitted Fruit van. The slatted vents in the ends are closed here but it also has two rows of three torpedo vents on the roof. Its wooden solebars and headstocks are fitted with original axleboxes and buffers and it runs on split spoked wheels. Note the tall vacuum pipes, off-centre V-hangers and the cast 'FRUIT' plate to the right of the door. Livery is weathered red oxide white white letters. E.B.

Plate 30. E141501 is an ex-LNER standard unfitted 12T van (COVAN B) to diagram 15, with sliding doors and an inspection hatch on the ends. It has a 9ft 0ins wheelbase steel chassis with Morton four shoe brake gear, split axleboxes and short four-web pattern buffers. One pair of disc and one pair of open spoked wheels give it a rather odd appearance. Built at Darlington in 1925, it was in grey livery with white lettering when photographed at St Albans City on 23rd May, 1949. E.B.

Plate 31. E166140 is an ex-LNER 12T goods van built to diagram 16 which has eight shoe vacuum brakes, open front axle boxes, standard buffers and tall vacuum pipes. It has an exterior sliding shutter on the end and its 9ft 0ins wheelbase chassis has wooden solebars and headstocks. The livery is weathered bauxite with small style white lettering. Photographed at Walsall, November 1957.   R.C.

Plate 32. E155963 is an ex-LNER diagram V43 Ventilated Fruit Van - from batch E155669-E156018. It has louvres low down on the ends as well as a loader's inspection hatch. Note the fruit-board clips above the '12T'. It has eight shoe vacuum brakes and webbed buffer housings all of LNER pattern - the short fillet on top of the buffer housing is for the shunter to rest his pole on when uncoupling. It has a 9ft 0ins wheelbase chassis, offset V-hangers and split spoked wheels. Livery is recorded as weathered red oxide with white lettering - the roof with its six torpedo vents is weathered white. Photographed at St Albans City, 25th February 1949.   E.B.

Plate 33. E179603 is an ex-LNER 12T wooden planked Fruit van on a 10ft 0ins wheelbase chassis with wooden solebars and headstocks. Built at Darlington in 1935, it started life as a diagram 94 ordinary ventilated van but was converted via diagram LNE165 by the addition of six torpedo roof ventilators and end slats. Note the asymmetrical eight shoe vacuum brake gear and the open front axleboxes of LNER pattern. Livery is weathered red oxide with white lettering and a weathered white roof. Photographed at Boxmoor, 15th April 1949.   E.B.

Plate 34. E229769 is an ex-LNER 10T Fish van with a 12ft 0in wheelbase chassis having eight shoe vacuum brakes. It is as built except for having BR plate front axleboxes and one pair of disc and one pair of split spoked wheels. Note the large end posts, tall vacuum pipe, small framed slate for chalked instructions and the cast plate 'FISH' along with the horizontal handrail on the door. Many of these were converted by BR to insulated Fish vans with new internal sliding doors (*see plate 3* etc.) and new livery. Photographed, April 1958.   R.C.

Plate 35. NE285714 is an ex-LNER 12T plywood-bodied Fruit van built to the final LNER fruit van design - diagram LNE187, (later perpetuated by BR as diagram 1/232) at Darlington in 1946. Note the end slats and two rows of three torpedo vents on the roof. It has a 10ft 0in wheelbase steel chassis, disc wheels, LNER style eight shoe vacuum brakes and 1ft 8½ins, four-rib spindle buffers. Livery was red oxide with white lettering, white roof, black solebars and below - the fitted fruit boards (above 'NE') read 'FRUIT ONLY/RETURN EMPTY TO/ MARCH OR PETERBOROUGH/LNE'. Photographed at Kings Langley, 28th August 1948. E.B.

Plate 36. (AD)E262364 is an ex-LNER diagram 172, 12T ventilated van with plywood body, Morton four shoe brakes, split axleboxes and tie bars. It has been vacuum braked by BR, circa 1958, and has self contained buffers. It is lettered 'LOAD TO BE/EVENLY DISTRIBUTED' (left) and 'NOT TO BE/LOOSE SHUNTED' (right) and coded ZRV above which it reads 'ER STORES/MATERIAL VAN/RETURN TO/DONCASTER WORKS'. Photographed at Doncaster Works, 1979. B.D.

Plate 37. E181497 photographed at Soho Pool Goods Depot, Birmingham in October 1957 is an ex-LNER diagram 25, 12T van with similar chassis features to the previous plate except for the buffers. Note the vertically planked wooden sides and corrugated steel ends - but no ventilators on the ends or the roof.

R.C.

Plate 38. E256948 - a van of similar design to diagram 25 but built to LNE diagram 116. The major difference between the two diagrams being the end ventilators and three part corrugated ends on diagram 116. Photographed at Marshmoor in the early 1970's. T.M.

Plate 39. E283257 is an ex-LNER 12T ventilated van built to diagram 195 at Darlington Works. It has a plywood body and a 10ft 0in wheelbase steel chassis with eight shoe vacuum brakes of LNER pattern. This diagram is essentially a vacuum braked version of diagram 172 *(see plate 36).* Photographed at Marshmoor in the early 1970's. T.M.

Plate 40. E284903 is from the same batch as *plate 39* (E283209-E285008) and is included as it has the later lettering style (coded VANFIT), split axleboxes and shows the tall vacuum pipes. Both *plates 39 and 40* have posters relating to the goods carried. Photographed at Marshmoor in the early 1970's. T.M.

Plate 41. E261500 is a 12T ex-LNER ventilated van of diagram 176 (E260949-E261548). A wartime design which features the unusual narrow vertical matchboard-type planking, it has Morton four shoe brakes being built unfitted but vacuum braked by BR post-1955. Note the U-channel diagonal side stanchions and the single metal end vents up to the top of the roof arc with metal plating at the top of the ends. There are two T-stanchions on the ends also. Photographed at Marshmoor in the early 1970's. T.M.

Plate 42. E284687 is an ex-LNER diagram 195, 12T ventilated van. It has eight shoe vacuum brakes, spindle buffers, LNER pattern open front axleboxes and tall vacuum pipes. It is one of two vans converted circa 1962, when they were given transparent sides and used for training purposes to demonstrate the correct way to load vans. At least one survived in internal use until the 1980's. B.R./D.L.

Plate 43. W144817 built by the SR to their diagram 1455 for the GWR (GW diagram V35) shows all the features common to this design *(see plates 20 and 21)*. It was built unfitted but was vacuum braked by BR, circa 1957, and has low vacuum pipes, spindle buffers, plate front axleboxes and tie bars. Photographed at Marshmoor in the early 1970's.   T.M.

Plate 44. W100389 is an ex-GWR 12T ventilated van, 'MINK A' built in 1923 to diagram V16. Its tare weight is 6t 10cwt and it is unfitted with GWR pattern self contained buffers and four shoe Dean-Churchward brake gear. Seen here in the 1960's when it had been condemned.   L.

Plate 45. W105078 is an ex-GWR 12T ventilated van, 'MINK A', built to diagram V16 and similar in many ways to the previous plate but the Dean-Churchward brake lever has been replaced by a Morton type and there are brakes on one side only. Note the rainstrip over the doors. Photographed, 1958.   L.

Plate 46. 064711 is an ex-GWR 10T 'MINK A', ventilated goods van with a horizontally planked wooden body with timber and angle iron bracing. It is unfitted with four shoe Dean-Churchward brake gear, (operated by a lever on the right), and has tie rods, self contained buffers, GWR pattern axleboxes and three link couplings. The small lettering reads 'For use at/STROUD/[CENTRAL]/only'. Photographed, when in internal use, at Gloucester Central on 31st July 1964.   R.S.

Plate 47. W93370 is an ex-GWR diagram Y4 10T Banana Van, being a circa 1921 conversion of a diagram X6 (1918) Meat van which was in itself a conversion from a diagram V16 ventilated van. The conversion to Y4 involved fitting the sliding vent in the centre of the ends (the other end vents being blanked off internally) and fitting an internal steam pipe. It is vacuum fitted and has Instanter couplings - its other chassis details being similar to the previous plate. Seen here in the 1960's when it had been condemned.   L.

Plate 48. W145743 is an ex-GWR 12T 'MINK A' ventilated goods van built to diagram V34, lot No. 1431. Virtually all these vans were vacuum braked by BR and had modified spindle buffers, tie bars, split axleboxes and it looks rather odd with one pair of disc and one pair of spoked wheels. It is easy to see how the BR Standard design evolved from this type of van by the addition of a corrugated end and a few other refinements. Photographed at St Blazey, 16th June 1958.   R.S.

Plate 49. W123971 is an ex-GWR 12T 'MOGO' of diagram G31, lot No. 1147 - a planked wooden bodied convertible goods van for motor car traffic - hence the end doors and flap with blocks to rest on the buffer housings. It has four shoe Morton vacuum brake gear and replacement plate front axleboxes. Note the rainstrip over the door has been removed. Photographed at Gloucester Central, 31st July 1964.   R.S.

Plate 50. 060080 is an ex-GWR 10T 'Iron Mink' of all-metal construction. It is unfitted with Morton style brake gear, GWR pattern oil axleboxes, early tapered spindle buffers and three link couplings. Seen here in internal use with a hatch in the roof for loading shavings. The small lettering reads 'For use at/Carr. Works only./For the conveyance of/shavings from/7 & 12 SHOPS/ to SAWMILLS'. Photographed at Swindon Works, September 1959.   R.S.

Plate 51. W146401 is an ex-GWR diagram V36, 12T plywood-bodied, ventilated goods van with Morton brake gear, (note the strengthening strip on the V-hanger). It has a three part rainstrip and is unfitted but was painted in brown livery with white lettering when photographed at Boxmoor on 15th April 1949. BR built identical vacuum braked vans to diagram 1/203. E.B.

Plate 52. M524876 is an ex-LMS diagram D2103 12T plywood-bodied ventilated goods van in use here as a Fish van. Built at Wolverton Works in 1945, it has a 10ft 0in wheelbase, eight shoe vacuum braked chassis with split axleboxes, spindle buffers and typical LMS J-hanger suspension. Note the tall vacuum pipes, four torpedo vents on the roof (in two rows), and the offset rainstrip. Photographed at Lowestoft on 18th September 1948 in bauxite livery with white lettering. E.B.

Plate 53. (AD)M216698 is an ex-LMS diagram D1814 12T van with horizontally planked sides and original pattern corrugated ends. It has standard LMS pattern eight shoe vacuum brakes (as did all this design) but no bracing to the sides. Photographed at Oxford, 8th October 1979.   B.D.

Plate 54. B750070 is a 12T ventilated goods van built to diagram 1/200, lot No. 2001, (1300 vans B750000-B751299) at BR Wolverton Works in 1949 to a design based on the LMS diagram D2108 *(see plate 14)*. Note the roof and the end vents, LMS style J-hanger suspension, three part corrugated ends and vertical and diagonal bracing to the plywood sides. Photographed at Marshmoor in the early 1970's.

                                                                                                                        T.M.

Plate 55. B850067 is a 12T goods van - Shock Absorbing, built to diagram 1/201, lot No. 2045, (one lot of 50 vans, B850050-B850099), at BR Faverdale, Darlington Works in 1948. It shows features similar to the last batch of LNER built fruit vans but has longitudinal springs, (under the protection bars) and buffers typical of Shock vans. The white squares on the sides (and ends) indicate shock absorbing. Note the 'Lowes Carta Carna Dog Food' label relating to a common traffic usage of these vans. Photographed at Maidstone West, Spring 1970. D.L.

Plate 56. B753188 is a 12T goods van, built to a GWR design at Swindon Works in 1949 - BR diagram 1/203, lot No. 2079, (100 vans, B753100-B753199). It has four shoe vacuum brake gear, tie bars, plate front axleboxes and spindle buffers. Note the absence of rainstrips on the roof. Photographed at Whittlesea, Autumn 1969. D.L.

Plate 57. B751405 is a diagram 1/204, lot No. 2003, (500 vans, B751300-B751799) 12T ventilated goods van. The design is based on LMS practice and these vans were built at BR Wolverton Works in 1949. It has the later pattern LMS corrugated ends (three part) and its brake gear, buffers etc are LMS style, *(see plates 12 and 13).* Photographed at Marshmoor in the early 1970's.   T.M.

Plate 58. B753331 originally designated a diagram 1/205, lot No. 2083, (one lot of 230 vans B753200-B753429) unfitted, 12T ventilated goods van. It was built in 1949 at BR Swindon Works but is here XP rated having had vacuum brakes and modified buffers - its other details are similar to *plate 56.* Note the three part rainstrip and the later 'boxed' style lettering. Photographed at Rochester, Winter 1968/69.   D.L.

Plate 59. B850000 is a 12T 'SHOCVAN' built to diagram 1/206, lot No. 2014, (one lot of 50 vans, B850000-B850049) at BR Wolverton Works in 1949 being basically a shock absorbing version of diagram 1/204 *(see plate 57)*. Photographed at Hoo Junction, Spring 1970. D.L.

Plate 60. B851814 is another SHOCVAN but built to diagram 1/209, lot No. 2471, (some 750 vans, B851600-B852349) at BR Faverdale, Darlington Works in 1949. This design was a shock absorbing version of the BR Standard van diagram 1/208 *(see plate 61)*. Note the later style of shock absorbing stripes - *plate 59* has the earlier style. Photographed at Marshmoor in the early 1970's. T.M.

Plate 61. B777387 is an ex-works, third pattern BR standard 12T ventilated goods van built to diagram 1/208, lot No. 3086, (850 vans, B777351-B778200) at BR Wolverton Works in 1958. It has BR eight shoe clasp vacuum brakes, screw couplings and self contained buffers. Note the split rainstrip, horizontally planked sides, plywood doors, two part corrugated ends, low vacuum pipes and absence of tie bars.

B.R./A.B.

Plate 62. B850563 is a 12T 'SHOCVAN' with plywood body and steel fittings. It was built in 1950 at BR Ashford Works to diagram 1/207, lot No. 2158, (500 vans in one lot only, B850100-B850599). Like many such vans it has Duplex type buffers, four shoe vacuum brakes, screw couplings, plate front axleboxes and tie bars. Seen here at Hoo Junction, Winter 1968/69. D.L.

Plate 63. B765001 is a standard 12T ventilated goods van built to diagram 1/208, lot No. 2367, (1000 vans, B764481-B765480) at BR Faverdale, Darlington Works in 1952. The standard plywood body with vertical and diagonal steel bracing and corrugated ventilated ends is mounted on a 10ft 0in wheelbase chassis which has Morton four shoe vacuum brakes, plate front axleboxes and tie bars. Note the central rainstrips over the doors. Photographed at Hoo Junction, Spring 1970. D.L.

Plate 64. B760065 was built to the same diagram as *plate 63* but to lot No. 2319, (1250 vans, B759180-B760429) at BR Wolverton Works in 1952. This 12T BR Standard van has wooden planked bodysides and three part, ventilated corrugated ends, Morton style four shoe vacuum brakes, tie bars and spindle buffers. Note one BR plate front axlebox *(left)* and an LNE open front type *(right)* along with one pair of disc and one pair of open spoked wheels. Photographed at Marshmoor in the early 1970's.   T.M.

Plate 65. (AD) B763525 is another diagram 1/208 12T standard van but of lot No. 2414, (750 vans, B763281-B764030) built at BR Wolverton Works in 1952. Although condemned and latterly in use as a stores van, it shows similar features to *plate 64*, but has two part corrugated ends and split axleboxes. The small lettering reads 'RETURN EMPTY TO /READING STORES /YARD, S&T/ READING'. Coded 'ZRV'   A.B.

Plate 66. B778893 (041257) is a 12T vacuum braked ventilated goods van - 'PALVAN' - of diagram 1/211, lot No. 3191, (300 vans, B778751-B779050), built at BR Faverdale, Darlington Works in 1959. Seen here late into its life and even condemned from restricted internal use, it shows all its original features. These vans rode badly at speed and despite restrictions, the problems continued and when some bad accidents were attributed to the design, they were largely removed from traffic. Photographed at Kings Lynn on 25th August 1977.   G.G.

Plate 67. WD41762 has similar body features to the van in the previous plate but its chassis has split axleboxes, hydraulic buffers and it runs on split spoked wheels. Note the reversing arrangement for the long handbrake lever with its extra supporting bracket and off centre V-hanger. Photographed at Leamington Spa General station in September 1964. Livery of these MOD vans was green with yellow lettering.   R.C.

Plate 68. B782867 is a 14T ventilated goods van - 'PALVAN', of diagram 1/223, lot No. 3373, (19 vans, B782854-B782872), built at BR Wolverton Works in 1960. The end stanchions extend below the headstocks to give added strength to the 20ft 0in long body with its four hinged doors down each side. Note the roller bearings and later pattern buffers on the eight shoe vacuum braked chassis. Photographed at Carlisle, Spring 1970.   D.L.

Plate 69. B854500 - the only one of its kind being built to diagram 1/215, lot No. 3292, (experimental lot 9001), at BR Derby Works in 1956. A shock absorbing 'PALVAN' with planked sides, two part corrugated ends and a conventional four shoe Morton vacuum braked chassis. Photographed at Wick, Summer 1970.   D.L

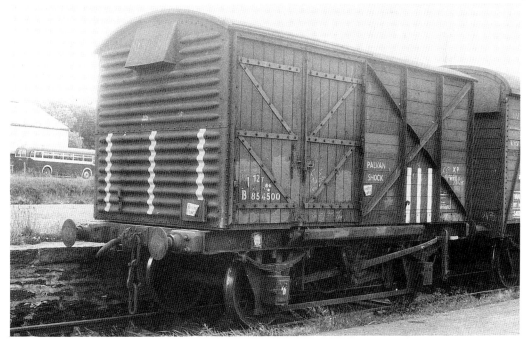

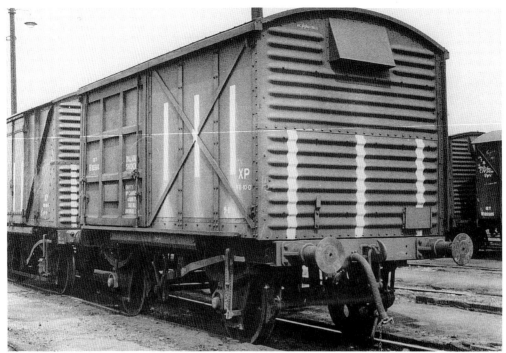

Plates 70 & 71. B855603 is a 12T ventilated, shock 'PALVAN' with plywood doors at the left of each side and corrugated ends. It was built to diagram 1/219, lot No. 3347, (125 vans, B855551-B855675) at BR Wolverton Works in December 1961. It has Oleo hydraulic buffers, roller bearings and eight shoe clasp vacuum brakes. The doors open by sliding to the right. The small lettering on the lower right hand panel of the doors reads:- 'EMPTY TO/Wm. CRAWFORD/ & SONS LTD/EDGEHILL/LIVERPOOL L.M.R.' - the van being used for biscuit traffic.   B.R./D.L.

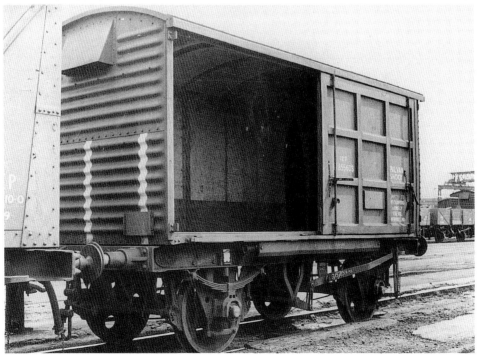

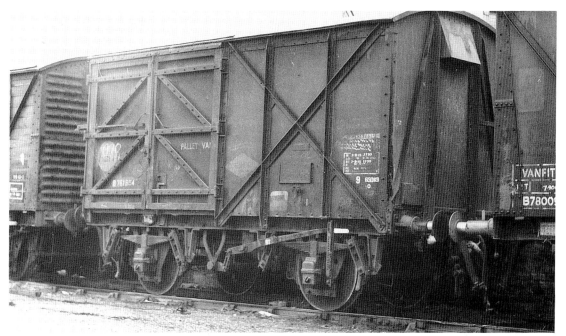

Plate 72. B781864 - built to the same diagram (1/211) as *plate 66* but to lot No. 3310, (522 vans, B781752-B782273), this PALVAN has similar details in body and basic chassis construction but it has been modified in an attempt to improve the riding qualities at speed. It has been given air brakes, friction link suspension and Oleo buffers similar to the ones fitted to the van in *plate 70*. It is one of seven vans so converted, others were B778971, B779026, B779834, B781763 and B781847/75. Photographed at Falkirk, Spring 1976. D.L.

Plate 73. B763280 is the only one of its kind being a 20T Pallet van with a 20ft 0in long body on a conventional 10ft 0in wheelbase vacuum braked chassis. It was built to diagram 1/229, lot No. 2696 at BR Faverdale, Darlington Works circa 1955 and has a part sheeted roof with cupboard doors on the sides. The steps and platform on the ends give access to the sheet roofing. B.R./D.L.

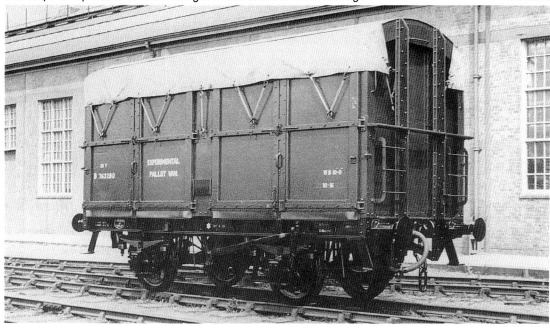

Plate 74. B782437 is a 12T ventilated goods van lettered PALVAN with a body which is just over 18ft long on an 10ft 0in wheelbase chassis. It was built to diagram 1/221, lot No. 3318, (one lot of 250 vans, B782274-B782523) at BR Derby Works in 1960. The body is made of plywood with flat wooden external bracing and a single vent in the ends. The doors slide outwards from the centre. It has Morton eight shoe vacuum brakes, roller bearings, Oleo buffers, screw couplings and LMS style J-hanger spring suspension. These vans were originally painted green and carried the name 'IZAL', and were lettered 'RETURN TO CHAPELTOWN, E.R.'. Photographed at Kings Lynn, Autumn 1969. D.L.

Plate 75. A 22T PALVAN built to diagram 1/235 with a 20ft 9ins wheelbase chassis and a body which is 35ft 0in over headstocks. The body is made of plywood with flat wooden battens on the sides but steel T section bracing on the ends. It has friction link suspension, air operated block brakes - being vacuum piped and fitted with a short central hand brake lever. Note the large diameter buffer heads, air brake and main reservoir pipes alongside the vacuum pipe on the ends and the Instanter couplings. These vans were originally painted blue and carried 'FORD' lettering, being used to carry car parts between Ford plants at Dagenham and Halewood. Some vans had their sides removed and replaced by blue p.v.c. sheeting. Photographed at Temple Mills, 1979. B.D.

Plate 76. B762361 is a 12T ventilated goods van built to diagram 1/212, lot No. 2585, (one lot of 150 vans, B762280-B762429) at BR Faverdale, Darlington Works in 1954. These vans were basically a diagram 1/208 standard design *(see plate 65)* which had 1ft 6ins Oleo hydraulic buffers and carried the lettering 'MARGARINE' on the 2 planks above the '12T', being designated for the transport of this commodity. Photographed at Whittlesea, Autumn 1969. D.L.

Plate 77. B772170, built at BR Faverdale, Darlington Works in 1955, is a diagram 1/213, lot No. 2855, (750 vans, B771451-B772200) 12T ventilated goods van with standard chassis details including 1ft 6ins spindle buffers. The vacuum cylinder and safety loops on the brake rods show up well. Note the single rainstrip over the doors and the lamp bracket on the three part corrugated end. Photographed at Hoo Junction, Spring 1970. D.L.

Plate 78. B776708 of the same diagram (1/213) as *plate 77* illustrates how variations can occur from one lot to another. This van of lot No. 3023, (800 vans, B776551-B777350) was built at BR Ashford Works in 1957 and differs from *plate 77* in having two part corrugated ends, split axleboxes and 1ft 8½ins spindle buffers. Photographed at Didcot, 1st November 1979. B.D.

Plate 79. B784314 is a 12T Ventilated Van built to diagram 1/217, lot No. 3392, (894 vans, B783873-B784766) at BR Derby Works in 1962. These vans had plywood double sliding doors and sides, with corrugated ends containing a central ventilator. They all had eight shoe vacuum brake gear as seen here. Note the heavy duty buffers and the plate front axleboxes. Photographed at Marshmoor in the early 1970's. T.M.

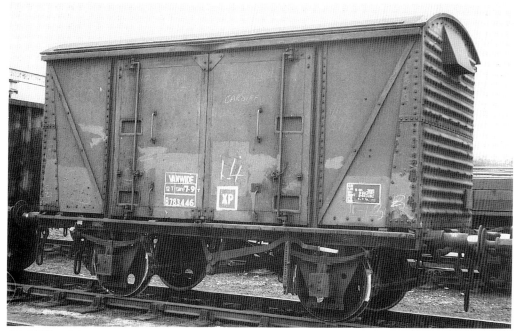

Plate 80. B783446 built at BR Wolverton Works in 1962 to the same diagram as *plate 79* (1/217) but to lot No. 3391, (1000 vans, B782873-B783872). This view shows the other side of the brake gear from *plate 79* and note the pneumatic buffers and the later 'boxed' lettering along with the intermediate code name 'VANWIDE'. Photographed at Hoo Junction, Spring 1969.   D.L.

Plate 81. B783802 has similar build data to *plate 80* but note the different buffers, split axleboxes, crudely stencilled number and the TOPS CODE VWV. Photographed at Acton, 16th November 1979.   B.D.

Plate 82. B780203 is a 12T goods van built to diagram 1/218, lot No.3109, (700 vans, B779851-B780550) at BR Ashford Works in 1958. It has plywood sides, corrugated ends, eight shoe vacuum brakes - note the offset V-hanger and the reversing arrangement for the brake lever. Note also the split axleboxes, low vacuum pipes, screw couplings and hydraulic buffers. Photographed at Didcot, 29th September 1979. B.D

Plate 83. B779954 of similar build details to *plate 82*, but showing the other side of the brake gear and plate front axleboxes. Note the various chalked instructions including 'DOWN LOAD TO READING 26/8' and 'Ely 25/8', all well away from the chalk boards provided. Photographed at Hoo Junction, Autumn 1968.   D.L.

Plate 84. B854527 is a SHOCVAN in disguise, built to diagram 1/218, lot No. 3117, (475 vans, B854526-B855000) at BR Faverdale, Darlington Works in 1958. Its body is similar to *plate 85* but its chassis no longer has the longitudinal shock springs - there is one central spring under the van floor giving increased safety but making maintenance difficult. Its other chassis details are similar to *plate 85* but it has pneumatic buffers. Photographed at Hoo Junction, Spring 1968.   D.L.

Plate 85. B854136 also built to diagram 1/218, but to lot No. 3008, (900 vans, B853600-B854499) at BR Faverdale, Darlington Works in 1957. Unlike *plate 84*, this van retains the conventional shock absorbing springs as well as Duplex buffers, Morton four shoe vacuum brakes, split axleboxes, tie bars and screw couplings. Note the 'boxed' style lettering and 'that' advertisement again! Photographed at Hoo Junction, Spring 1968.   D.L.

Plate 86. B852900 is a 12T plywood-sided SHOCVAN with two part corrugated steel ends and showing full 'shock livery'. It was built to diagram 1/209, lot No. 2865, (700 vans, B852900-B853599) at BR Faverdale, Darlington Works in August 1956. Note the white lettering on the black patch -'EMPTY TO/EASTERN OR/NORTH EASTERN REGION'. It has Morton four shoe vacuum brakes, Duplex buffers, plate front axleboxes, tie bars and Instanter couplings.

B.R./A.B.

Plate 87. B853509 has the same build data as *plate 86* but note the split axleboxes and the lettering - 'S.R./SHOCVAN'. Photographed at Northampton, Spring 1970. D.L.

Plate 88. B855033 is a 12T shock absorbing goods van built to diagram 1/220, lot No. 3224, (one lot of 100 vans, B855001-B855100) at BR Faverdale, Darlington Works in 1959. It is very similar to *plate 84* but has external shock springs and Duplex buffers. It also has the earlier style of shock stripes, although they are missing from the end *(see plate 86 for comparison)*. Photographed at Hoo Junction, Winter 1969/70.

D.L.

Plate 89. (AD)B786548 is a diagram 1/224, lot No. 3398, (one massive lot of 2000 vans, B784873-B786872)van built by Pressed Steel in 1961. These 12T ventilated goods vans were similar to the vans of diagram 1/213 *(see plates 77 and 78).* Note the absence of tie bars, the coding ZRV and the pneumatic buffers. Now alas condemned, it awaits its fate!   A.B.

Plate 90. B875021 is a 12T goods van lettered 'FRUIT', built to an LMS design under BR diagram 1/230, lot No. 2018, (200 vans, B875000-B875199) at BR Wolverton Works in 1949. It has plywood sides with air scoops just above the solebars, three part corrugated ends with ventilators. Other features show clear LMS affinity, such as the axleguards, springing and brake gear. Photographed at Hoo Junction, Spring 1968.   D.L.

Plate 91. E277892 is an ex-LNER diagram 187, plywood-bodied fruit van with end slats but lacking roof ventilators that were originally fitted *(see plate 35)*. It has LNER style eight shoe vacuum brakes, spindle buffers, split axleboxes and tall vacuum pipes. Photographed at Marshmoor in the early 1970's.   T.M.

Plate 92. B755165 is a 12T diagram 1/232, lot No. 2134, (one lot only of 750 vans, B754430-B755179) fruit van, lettered 'FRUIT' on a cast iron plate on the door. This BR diagram was a continuation of LNER diagram 187 as can be seen by comparison with the above plate. This van has plate front and split axleboxes, low vacuum pipes and no chalking plate but otherwise the two vans are very similar. Photographed at Whittlesea, Autumn 1969.   D.L.

Plate 93. B875503 closely resembling *plate 91*, has the same build details but is from lot No. 2135, (250 vans, B875300-B875549) and was produced at BR Faverdale, Darlington Works in 1950 closely following the LMS design. Note the LNE pattern vacuum brakes used on this batch. Photographed at Marshmoor in the early 1970's.   T.M.

Plate 94. B875726 is a diagram 1/233, lot No.2738, (100 vans B875650-B875749) van built at BR Faverdale, Darlington Works in 1955. This design closely resembles diagram 1/213 *(see plates 77 and 78)* but the body has the air scoops like *plate 90*, and internal shelving was fitted. Photographed at Marshmoor in the early 1970's.   T.M.

Plate 95. B875287 based on GWR diagram Y8 (seen here ex-works) is a 12T Fruit van, built to diagram 1/231, lot No. 2084, (one lot of 100 vans, B875200-B875299) at BR Swindon Works in 1949. It has two vents in each plywood end as well as louvred sides with plywood doors. The safety loops show up well on the four shoe vacuum brake gear and it has split axleboxes, spindle buffers, tie bars and Instanter couplings. Note the ratchet brake lever bracket.

B.R./A.B.

Plate 96. B880680, built to diagram 1/242, lot No. 2598, (50 vans, B880680-B880729) at BR Faverdale, Darlington Works and seen there in 1954, is an 8T Banana van of the last diagram to have steam heating. It has Morton four shoe vacuum brakes, split axleboxes, tie bars, open spoked wheels and spindle buffers. Note the short end stanchions, central end lamp bracket and the flush fitting doors on the vertical planked wooden body.

B.R./A.B.

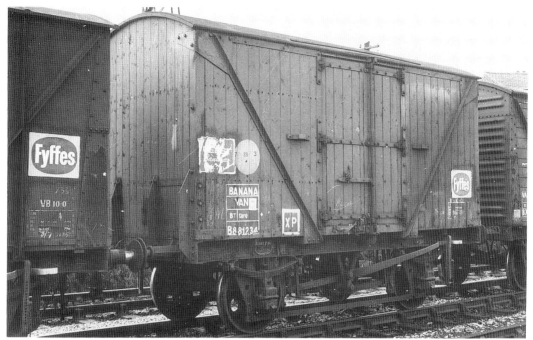

Plate 97. B881234 is an 8T Banana van built to diagram 1/243, lot No. 3010, (one lot only of 230 vans, B881130-B881359) at BR Faverdale, Darlington Works in 1957. The steam heating has been replaced by through steam pipes along the chassis and the side and end stanchions have been made much more robust compared to *plate 96*. Note the painting in black of the tare weight on the yellow spot which identifies the class. Photographed at Lostock Hall, Spring 1968.   D.L.

Plate 98. B881548 is a diagram 1/244, lot No. 3119, (250 vans, B881360-B881609) 8T Banana van built in 1958 at BR Faverdale, Darlington Works. This design has eight shoe vacuum brake gear and 2ft 0½ins Oleo hydraulic buffers. Only through steam pipes were fitted and note how the roof has little overhang. Photographed at Hoo Junction, Spring 1968.   D.L.

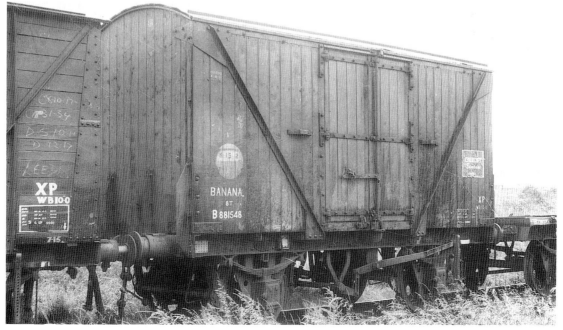

Plate 99. B882117 - clearly based on the BR standard design - is a 12T Banana van built to diagram 1/246, lot No. 3225, (227 vans, B882010-B882236) at BR Faverdale, Darlington Works in 1959. It is unventilated and later developments in Banana van design include plywood sides, eight shoe clasp vacuum brakes (note the offset V-hangers) and Oleo buffers. These vans were merely insulated and fitted with a through steam pipe - they had no steam heating. Photographed at Exeter (Newham), Spring 1970.

D.L.

Plate 100. B872094 started life as a 10T insulated meat van built to diagram 1/251, lot No. 2321, (200 vans, B872000-B872199) at BR Wolverton Works in 1952. Clearly derived from diagram 1/208 - the only obvious difference being the lack of end vents *(see plate 65).* With the reduction in meat traffic, these vans were put to other uses as here - for carrying ALE. It still shows signs of its original meat van livery though! Photographed at Weymouth, Spring 1970.

D.L.

Plate 101. B872056 has the same build details as *plate100* but is seen here as new in white livery - the lettering, solebars and below being painted in black. The paint date on the solebar reads 28-3-1953, which is when the van was out-shopped as new.

B.R./A.B.

Plate 102. B870006 is a 10T ventilated meat van lettered 'MEAT/(FOR FRESHMEAT)' which was built to diagram 1/250, lot No. 2320, (100 vans, B870000-B870099) at BR Wolverton Works in 1952. Again it closely relates to diagram 1/208 but has a row of four vents down the centre of the corrugated ends and louvred vents on either side of the doors. It has Morton four shoe vacuum brakes, tie bars, split axleboxes, spindle buffers and spoked wheels and was photographed when new. B.R./A.B.

Plate 103. B882409 is another 12T Banana van to the same diagram as *plate 99* but to lot No. 3290, (400 vans, B882238-B882637) built at BR Wolverton Works in 1960. Note the split axleboxes, the lamp brackets picked out in white on the end and the lack of ventilators. The crudely painted lettering on the door shows the van's new use for which it is coded RBV. Photographed at Oxford station, 5th September 1979. B.D.

Plate 104. B784287 is a 12T Ventilated van built to diagram 1/234, lot No. 3392, (6 vans only, B784285-B784290) at BR Derby Works in 1962. It is similar to the VANWIDES of diagram 1/217 *(see plates 79, 80 and 81)* but has no ventilators in the ends, having two Continental-style shuttered ventilators, one in each door instead, thought to be associated with the conveyance of market garden produce such as tomatoes but has never been confirmed. B.R./D.L.

These notes were prepared with grateful thanks to David Larkin.

Page 5 :   The date of the photograph should be 4th May 1962.

Page 10: The lettering section. The boxed style dates from circa 1964 and not the late 1950's. TOPS codes were added to lettering styles of both periods.

Page 11: Plate 1. This vehicle is an 8 plank wagon.

Page 15: Plate 9. This vehicle was vacuum braked by BR post 1955. In this particular case, the Oleo buffers date the conversion as circa 1959. The livery is weathered bauxite.

Page 18: Plate 16. This also differs from LNE practice in having floorboards mounted directly onto the solebar, thus making the body higher.

Page 20: Plate 20. There were 140 PRESTWIN's, not 40, and they were not for cement. Loads include sand, as shown and alumina.

Page 21: Plate 22. The container is LNE - built to Diagram 33, batch A1037E to A1336E.

Page 23: Plate 25. Number is M707102.

Page 25: Plate 30. Number is DE281943.

Page 27: Plate 34. Lot No. 2798 (2000 wagons B251609 - B253608).

Page 29: Plate 38. This vehicle is a Diagram 1/109.

Page 32: Plate 43. Loco Coal wagons were originally painted black with white lettering and this vehicle carries that livery. Date of change to grey not known.

Pages 34 & 38: Plates 48 & 54. This livery is known as Freight Brown and not Bauxite, which was a different shade altogether. A few examples appeared circa 1964 but the main use was from about 1977 onwards for rebodied stock, as shown.

Pages 36 & 37: Plates 50 - 52. North Blyth *not* North Blythe.

Page 56: Plate 91. This vehicle has had the stanchions cut down for a special newsprint load, as shown. In some captions 'rivetted' appears incorrectly with only one 't'.

Locations and dates (unknown at the time of publication) for some of the photographs used in Profile No.1

Plate 6: Doncaster, Summer 1969. *Plate 10:* Hoo Junction, Winter 1968/69. *Plate 13:* Rochester, Winter 1968/69. *Plate 14:* Hoo Junction, Winter 1968/69. *Plate16:* Hoo Junction, Spring 1968. *Plate 18:* Brierley Hill, Spring 1978. *Plate 20:* Congleton, Summer 1968. *Plate 32:* Crumlin, Spring 1972. *Plate 36:* Strood, Spring 1968. *Plate 38:* Hoo Junction, Autumn 1970. *Plate 53:* Doncaster, Summer 1969. *Plate 59:* Hoo Junction, Spring 1970. *Plate 60:* Marks Tey, Winter 1969/70. *Plate 62:* Ryburgh, Autumn 1969. *Plate 68:* Hoo Junction, Spring 1968. *Plate 69:* Corby, Autumn 1969. *Plate 70:* Wigston, Spring 1970.

Back cover:

Top Left: 064526 (its internal user number) is an ex-GWR 10T 'Iron Mink' van. It has similar build details to *plate 50* but the faded body colour is unusual and has led to the appearance of 'G' and 'W' through the later paint finish. Photographed at Fishguard in 1966.   C.R.

Lower Left: DM523505 was built by the Southern Railway in 1944 for the LMS who gave these 12T vans diagram number D2078, this one being of Lot No. 1373, (250 vans, M523290-M523539). Built unfitted, it has been vacuum braked and fitted with replacement buffers by BR. The planking on the end and to the left of the door has largely been replaced but more of the characteristic mixed pattern is seen to the right of the door, *see plate 21.* The Southern Railway also built vans to this design for the GWR. Photographed at Bowes Park in Autumn 1974 when in use on electrification work.   P.W.

Top Right: 083029 (ex-DW142357) is an ex-GWR 12T van to diagram V24. It has Morton four shoe brake gear but has been vacuum fitted by BR along with buffer modifications. Other features include plate front axleboxes, tie bars, screw couplings and three-hole disc wheels. The condemned sign sees it languishing at the end of a siding awaiting its fate when photographed at Andover in Spring 1986.   P.W.

Bottom Right: E87675 is an ex-12T INSUL-FISH van built to the second BR design (E87500-E88057). Note how the bracing on the sides differs from that on the earlier designs *(see plates 2,3 and 4)* and how the ends have the added diagonal bracing. It has Oleo type buffers but has the same brake gear and bearings as *plate 6* - many such vans were subsequently classified as Special Parcels Vans when fish traffic declined. This van still retains its Rail Blue livery but it had passed into departmental use as QRV ADB975965 when photographed at Bounds Green in April 1987.   P.W.